POCKET
prayers
for FRIENDS

POCKET
prayers
for FRIENDS

40 SIMPLE PRAYERS THAT BRING
JOY AND SERENITY

Max Lucado

with Betsy St. Amant

THOMAS NELSON
Since 1798

Published in Nashville, Tennessee, by Thomas Nelson. Thomas Nelson is a registered trademark of HarperCollins Christian Publishing, Inc.

Thomas Nelson titles may be purchased in bulk for educational, business, fund-raising, or sales promotional use. For information, please e-mail SpecialMarkets@ThomasNelson.com.

Unless otherwise noted, Scripture quotations are taken from the New King James Version®. © 1982 by Thomas Nelson. Used by permission. All rights reserved.

Scripture quotations marked NCV are from the New Century Version®. © 2005 by Thomas Nelson. Used by permission. All rights reserved.

Scripture quotations marked NIV are from the Holy Bible, New International Version®, NIV®. Copyright © 1973, 1978, 1984, 2011 by Biblica, Inc.® Used by permission of Zondervan. All rights reserved worldwide. www.zondervan.com. The "NIV" and "New International Version" are trademarks registered in the United States Patent and Trademark Office by Biblica, Inc.®

Scripture quotations marked NLT are from the Holy Bible, New Living Translation. © 1996, 2004, 2007, 2013 by Tyndale House Foundation. Used by permission of Tyndale House Publishers, Inc., Carol Stream, Illinois 60188. All rights reserved.

Any Internet addresses, phone numbers, or company or product information printed in this book are offered as a resource and are not intended in any way to be or to imply an endorsement by Thomas Nelson, nor does Thomas Nelson vouch for the existence, content, or services of these sites, phone numbers, companies, or products beyond the life of this book.

ISBN 978-0-7180-7837-9 (eBook)

Library of Congress Control Number: 2015956804
ISBN 978-0-7180-7738-9

Printed in Mexico

17 18 19 20   RRD   10 9 8 7 6 5 4 3 2

The Pocket Prayer

Hello, my name is Max. I'm a recovering prayer wimp. I doze off when I pray. My thoughts zig, then zag, then zig again. Distractions swarm like gnats on a summer night. If attention deficit disorder applies to prayer, I am afflicted. When I pray, I think of a thousand things I need to do. I forget the one thing I set out to do: pray.

Some people excel in prayer. They inhale heaven and exhale God. They are the SEAL Team Six of intercession. They would rather pray than sleep. Why is it that I sleep when I pray? They belong to the PGA: Prayer Giants Association. I am a card-carrying member of the PWA: Prayer Wimps Anonymous.

Can you relate? It's not that we don't pray at all. We all pray some.

On tearstained pillows we pray.

In grand liturgies we pray.

At the sight of geese in flight, we pray.

Quoting ancient devotions, we pray.

We pray to stay sober, centered, or solvent. We pray when the lump is deemed malignant. When the money runs out before the month does. When the unborn baby hasn't kicked in a while. We all pray . . . some.

But wouldn't we all like to pray . . .

More?

Better?

Deeper?

Stronger?

With more fire, faith, or fervency?

Yet we have kids to feed, bills to pay, deadlines to meet.

The calendar pounces on our good intentions like a tiger on a rabbit. We want to pray, but *when*?

We want to pray, but *why*? We might as well admit it. Prayer is odd, peculiar. Speaking into space. Lifting words into the sky. We can't even get the cable company to answer us, yet God will? The doctor is too busy, but God isn't? We have our doubts about prayer.

And we have our checkered history with prayer: unmet expectations, unanswered requests. We can barely genuflect for the scar tissue on our knees. God, to some, is the ultimate heartbreaker. Why keep tossing the coins of our longings into a silent pool? He jilted me once . . . but not twice.

Oh, the peculiar puzzle of prayer.

We aren't the first to struggle. The sign-up sheet for Prayer 101 contains some familiar names: the apostles John, James, Andrew, and Peter. When one of Jesus' disciples requested, "Lord, teach us to pray" (Luke 11:1 NIV), none of the others objected. No one walked away saying, "Hey, I have prayer figured out." The first followers of Jesus needed prayer guidance.

The first followers of Jesus needed prayer guidance.

In fact, the only tutorial they ever requested was on prayer. They could have asked for instructions on many topics: bread multiplying, speech making, storm stilling. Jesus raised people from the dead. But a "How to Vacate the Cemetery" seminar? His followers never called for one. But they did want him to do this: "Lord, teach us to pray."

Might their interest have had something to do with the jaw-dropping, eye-popping promises Jesus attached to prayer? "Ask and it will be given to you" (Matt. 7:7 NIV). "If you believe, you will get anything you ask for in prayer" (Matt. 21:22 NCV). Jesus never attached such power to other endeavors. "*Plan* and it will be given to you." "You will get anything you *work* for." Those words are not in the Bible. But these are—"If you remain in me and follow my teachings, you can ask anything you want, and it will be given to you" (John 15:7 NCV).

Jesus gave stunning prayer promises.

And he set a compelling prayer example. Jesus prayed before he ate. He prayed for children. He prayed for the sick. He prayed with thanks. He prayed with tears. He had made the planets and shaped the stars, yet he prayed. He is the Lord of angels and Commander of heavenly hosts, yet he prayed. He is coequal with God, the exact representation of the Holy One, and yet he devoted himself to prayer. He prayed in the desert, cemetery, and garden. "He went out and departed to a solitary place; and there He prayed" (Mark 1:35).

This dialogue must have been common among his friends:

"Has anyone seen Jesus?"

"Oh, you know. He's up to the same thing."

"Praying *again*?"

"Yep. He's been gone since sunrise."

Jesus would even disappear for an entire night of prayer. I'm thinking of one occasion in particular. He'd just experienced one of the most stressful days of his ministry. The day began with the news of the death of his relative John the Baptist. Jesus sought to retreat with his disciples, yet a throng of thousands followed him. Though grief-stricken, he spent the day teaching and healing people. When it was discovered that the host of people had no food to eat, Jesus multiplied bread out of a basket and fed the entire multitude. In the span of a few hours, he battled sorrow, stress, demands, and needs. He deserved a good night's rest. Yet when evening finally came, he told the crowd to leave and the disciples to board their boat, and "he went up into the hills by himself to pray" (Mark 6:46 NLT).

Apparently it was the correct choice. A storm exploded over the Sea of Galilee, leaving the disciples "in trouble far away from land, for a strong wind had risen, and they were fighting heavy waves. About three o'clock in the morning Jesus came toward them, walking on the water" (Matt. 14:24–25 NLT). Jesus ascended the mountain depleted. He reappeared invigorated. When he reached the water, he never broke his stride. You'd have thought the water was a park lawn and the storm a spring breeze.

Do you think the disciples made the prayer–power connection? "Lord, teach us to pray *like that*. Teach us to find strength in prayer. To banish fear in prayer. To defy storms in prayer. To come off the mountain of prayer with the authority of a prince."

What about you? The disciples faced angry waves and a watery grave. You face angry clients, a turbulent economy, raging seas of stress and sorrow.

"Lord," we still request, "teach us to pray."

When the disciples asked Jesus to teach them to pray, he gave them a prayer. Not a lecture on prayer. Not the doctrine of prayer. He gave them a quotable, repeatable, portable prayer (Luke 11:1–4).

Could you use the same? It seems to me that the prayers of the Bible can be distilled into one. The result is a simple, easy-to-remember, pocket-size prayer:

Father,
   you are good.
      I need help. Heal me and forgive me.
     They need help.
     Thank you.
     In Jesus' name, amen.

Let this prayer punctuate your day. As you begin your morning, *Father, you are good.* As you commute to work or walk the hallways at school, *I need help.* As you wait in the grocery line, *They need help.* Keep this prayer in your pocket as you pass through the day.

When we invite God into our world, he walks in. He brings

a host of gifts: joy, patience, resilience. Anxieties come, but they don't stick. Fears surface and then depart. Regrets land on the windshield, but then comes the wiper of prayer. The devil still hands me stones of guilt, but I turn and give them to Christ.

I'm completing my sixth decade, yet I'm wired with energy. I am happier, healthier, and more hopeful than I have ever been. Struggles come, for sure. But so does God.

Prayer is not a privilege for the pious, not the art of a chosen few. Prayer is simply a heartfelt conversation between God and his child. My friend, he wants to talk with you. Even now, as you read these words, he taps at the door. Open it. Welcome him in. Let the conversation begin.

> *Prayer is not a privilege for the pious, not the art of a chosen few. Prayer is simply a heartfelt conversation between God and his child.*

Prayers for Grace
and Wisdom

1

Plans go wrong for lack of advice;
many advisers bring success.

PROVERBS 15:22 NLT

Father God, I praise you for who you are and what you mean to me. You are so good in all your ways, and your Word tells me that you are my wonderful Counselor.

I ask you for wisdom today. Let it flow out of me and into my friendships. Help me not only to seek wise counsel but also to heed it.

Please guide my friends on their journeys today. Help them seek you always. Let their paths be made straight and sure.

Thank you for being a constant presence in my life. Your advice is trustworthy, and I can rest in it, realizing you want the best for me. I am grateful for friends who encourage me with your wisdom and truth.

In your Son's name I pray, amen.

2

He who walks with wise men will be wise, but
the companion of fools will be destroyed.

Proverbs 13:20

Almighty God, you sent your Son as an example of love, holiness, and wisdom. I praise you for that.

Help me reflect your love and embrace the wisdom you offer. I ask you to bring healthy friendships into my life and to protect me from relationships that would pull me away from you.

Bring positive influences into the lives of my friends. Equip them to sharpen each other to become more like you every day.

Thank you for caring about every aspect of my life, especially the people in it. And thank you for continuing to open doors to relationships that honor you.

In the name of Jesus, amen.

3

---

*Do not be deceived: "Evil company
corrupts good habits."*

1 CORINTHIANS 15:33

Heavenly Father, I praise you for your constant involvement in my life. You never fail to meet all my needs and to lead me in truth.

I need discernment today regarding the friendships I allow in my life. Give me wisdom to know which relationships to embrace and which ones to pass by.

I ask you to guide my friends in this too. Protect them from negative influences that might draw them away from your presence.

Thank you for being a constant friend. Even in temporary seasons of loneliness, you're with me. I'm so grateful for your presence when other relationships are in transition.

In Jesus' name, amen.

4

_____

_He said to me, "My grace is sufficient
for you, for my power is made perfect in
weakness." Therefore I will boast all the
more gladly about my weaknesses, so
that Christ's power may rest on me._

2 CORINTHIANS 12:9 NIV

Dear Lord, you alone are worthy. You're the only one who can meet me exactly where I am. Your grace is all I truly need.

Some days I struggle to embrace that truth even though I believe it. I need help holding on to you when circumstances try to convince me otherwise. Give me wisdom to understand your power, grace, and provision in the days they feel out of reach.

Help my friends recognize your provision even in the hard times. Let them always sense your presence, support, and love. Pour your grace into their lives, and make them strong.

Thank you for always meeting my needs, just as your Word promises. On the days when my patience runs thin and my heart breaks, your grace is still enough to cover all the messes of life.

In the name of your powerful Son, Jesus, amen.

5

---

*I commend you to God and to the word
of His grace, which is able to build
you up and give you an inheritance
among all those who are sanctified.*

ACTS 20:32

Dear Father God, I praise you for who you are. You are generous and compassionate to your children.

Some days I feel lost and unsure. Help me go to your Word and understand its truth. Use your Word to build me up and strengthen me every day.

Prompt my friends to read your Word and to commit it to memory so they will always have access to your promises. Give them a desire to study the Bible together and to strengthen each other with your instructions.

Thank you for the Bible. Thank you for the friendships that encourage me to be a student of the Word and to be committed to you.

In the powerful name of Jesus, amen.

6

---

*Let us consider one another in order
to stir up love and good works.*

HEBREWS 10:24

Almighty God, I praise you for your good heart toward your children. Even when I fail, your love never does. You are worthy to be praised.

Help me to be mindful of my motives. When I serve others, let it be out of genuine kindness and not selfishness, giving you all the glory. I want to set an example and encourage others toward good works. Help me show my friends true love and humility.

Please be with my friends as they strive to live for you. Help them stir one another toward good things. Let their hearts be focused on you alone.

Thank you that your love for me doesn't depend on my works but on your grace alone. Thank you for my friends, who remind me with their wisdom and joy of your many blessings. I'm so grateful we can work together and bring you glory.

In your holy and precious Son's name, amen.

Prayers for Joy and Companionship

7

Two people are better off than one, for they can help each other succeed. If one person falls, the other can reach out and help. But someone who falls alone is in real trouble.

ECCLESIASTES 4:9–10 NLT

Gracious Father, every good and perfect gift comes from you, especially the friendships you've given me. I praise you for your attention to every detail of my life, including relationships.

I want to be strong for my friends when they go through trials and storms. Help me pick them up and point them toward you in every situation. Enable me to laugh with them as they rejoice and cry beside them as they struggle.

My friends have been such blessings to me. I ask that you give them strength for their days, whatever season they're in, and guard their steps. If they falter, don't let them fall.

Thank you for the gift of friendship. I'm so grateful for the joy and companionship my friends bring. You never fail to provide just what I need—like people who draw me closer to you.

In your gracious name, amen.

8

Ointment and perfume delight the heart,
and the sweetness of a man's friend
gives delight by hearty counsel.

PROVERBS 27:9

Dear Lord, your presence is like a sweet perfume drifting over my life. I praise you for your goodness and provision! You are worthy to be praised.

I ask you to prepare me today so I might be a sweet aroma for my friends. I want to bless them as they continually bless me. Help me to be aware of their needs and to focus on them, putting my own agenda aside.

Equip my friends today to rest in your presence, lingering there and being refreshed in you. Let them find their full delight in your love today.

Thank you for the sweetness of friendship. Laughter and late-night talks refresh my spirit and fill me with joy.

In Jesus' name, amen.

9

*Rejoice with those who rejoice, and
weep with those who weep.*

Romans 12:15

Father God, you know every hair on my head and every word before it leaves my mouth. My days were written out before I was born. I praise you for your deep knowledge of me. You know what makes me happy, what makes me sad, and what hurts me. You bottle my tears.

Help me not to be selfishly caught up in my own joys and sorrows but to be a friend who cries when my friends cry and laughs when they laugh. Bonds are created through shared tears and laughter, and I want to be a good friend to my friends.

Be with them as they experience both joy and sorrow. When they're full of joy, let that passion bubble over and strengthen our friendship. When they hurt, let them feel your presence, and let them know I am here for them.

Thank you for the friends who laugh with me, celebrate with me, and encourage me. Thank you for those heart-to-heart talks that draw us closer to each other and to you.

In your Son's holy name, amen.

10

---

*A person finds joy in giving an apt reply—
and how good is a timely word!*

PROVERBS 15:23 NIV

Dear Lord God, you are the giver of words. I praise you for that gift. You blessed me with the ability to speak to my friends' hearts.

May I always remember that a kind word spoken at the right time can bring hope to a friend with a broken heart. Tame my tongue so I will speak only encouraging words.

Help my friends use their words wisely and carefully. When they're tempted to spout off in fear, doubt, or anger, remind them to be gentle. Guide their words so they will spread joy.

Thank you for friends who lift me up, encourage me, and speak your truth into my life. Thank you for providing me with so many loved ones who use their words to heal and not to hurt. I'm very grateful for them.

In the name of Jesus Christ, amen.

11

We took sweet counsel together, and
walked to the house of God in the throng.

PSALM 55:14

Heavenly Father, I love going to church to worship you, to learn more about your character, and to fellowship with other believers. You have provided me a community of believers where I can grow in your grace.

Let me be a sweet encouragement to my friends at church to draw closer to you. Help me be free with my worship and not hold back so they might also have the courage to express themselves freely.

Help my friends attend church faithfully and grow alongside me as we worship you together. Stretch and develop their faith as they learn more about you.

I love learning about you through fellowship with my friends. Thank you for that opportunity and for the friendships you've given me in my church. It's such a gift to worship beside them.

In your sweet name, amen.

12

---

*When my father and my mother forsake
me, then the Lord will take care of me.*

Psalm 27:10

Almighty God, you are a constant in my life. I praise you for your faithfulness. Even if everyone around me fails, you never do. I can always count on your presence.

Equip me to trust you in new ways and to greater depths. Help me release any fears I'm carrying, and remind me that you have never left me and will never forsake me. In turn, I want to be someone my friends can trust and depend on at all times.

Bless my friends with your presence when they struggle with loneliness. Be the companion they seek. Pursue their hearts, and reassure them that they are never alone, because you are always there.

Thank you for the gift of your constant presence. Thank you for the joy of friendship and the companionship it brings.

In the powerful name of Jesus, amen.

13

And Jesus came and spoke to them, saying, "All authority has been given to Me in heaven and on earth. Go therefore and make disciples of all the nations, baptizing them in the name of the Father and of the Son and of the Holy Spirit, teaching them to observe all things that I have commanded you; and lo, I am with you always, even to the end of the age."

MATTHEW 28:18–20

Heavenly Father, I praise you for the opportunities we have to spread the good news of the gospel. You are so loving, and you desire that everyone in the world would hear about your Son, Jesus.

Help me to partner with my friends in spreading the word about salvation and to speak about my faith plainly and simply. Prompt me to follow through when I hesitate to share your love with those I meet.

Give my friends courage as they seek to share your love with those who haven't heard of you. Provide them clarity as they talk about you, and inspire them to be strong witnesses motivated by love for your children.

Thank you for the opportunity to stand alongside my friends as we tell others about your grace. It's a joy to serve your kingdom together.

In Jesus' name, amen.

Prayers for Help
and Protection

14

---

*A friend loves at all times, and a
brother is born for adversity.*

PROVERBS 17:17

Heavenly Father, you are the very definition of love. I praise you for the many ways you show your love for me—through music, through your creation, and through the people you've placed in my life.

Help me reflect that love to others, especially my friends. Provide opportunities for me to be there for them in good times and bad and to encourage them through hugs, small gestures of kindness, and messages of hope, as they have done for me.

Strengthen my friends for whatever they're facing. Help them shine your love into all circumstances—even when it's hard or messy. Give them everything they need today, and provide them with an extra measure of grace.

Thank you for the blessing of friendships saturated in your love. I'm so grateful we don't have to navigate life on our own.

In Jesus' name, amen.

15

Those who wait on the LORD shall renew their strength; they shall mount up with wings like eagles, they shall run and not be weary, they shall walk and not faint.

ISAIAH 40:31

God of wonders, I praise you for who you are and how you take care of me. You always provide me with strength when I'm weak and perseverance when I feel as if I can't continue. You are so good to me.

Give me strong legs and determination as I run this race. Keep me moving forward even when the trail is bumpy and unsure. Lengthen my strides of faith, and prepare me to carry on when I'm scared or when all seems lost.

Help my friends find their strength in you during their rocky times. Let them spread their wings and fly despite adversity. Renew their energy daily, and give them your peace and comfort when they're struggling to keep going.

Thank you for always giving me what I need. I am so grateful for the friends who run beside me and help me persevere.

In the precious name of Jesus, amen.

16

---

*Fear not, for I am with you; be not dismayed,
for I am your God. I will strengthen
you, yes, I will help you, I will uphold
you with My righteous right hand.*

Isaiah 41:10

Heavenly Father, I praise you for your protection. Fear is a real battle, yet you tell me that perfect love casts out fear.

It is easy for me to fall into the trap of fear. Teach me to trust in you. You are my strength and my portion, and I have no reason to be afraid. But in those moments when fear seems inevitable, equip me with a clear perspective, and remind me that I won't have to face it alone.

Be with my friends and help them find courage in the midst of their fears. Enable them to fight depression and discouragement through your strength.

Thank you for being my hero and my protector. You're my safety net in an unsafe world, and I am so grateful you are always for me. Thank you for friends who encourage me to trust you.

In the name of Jesus, amen.

17

The LORD shall preserve you from all evil;
He shall preserve your soul. The LORD shall
preserve your going out and your coming in
from this time forth, and even forevermore.

PSALM 121:7-8

Dear Lord, this world is so uncertain. Yet you are good in the midst of the evil. I praise you for your love and protection.

When the world gets especially dark, help me trust you and look for your light and not be afraid of the shadows. I want always to remember how close you are to me. You're my refuge. Help me encourage my friends and those around me with that truth.

When my friends face trials—sickness, broken relationships, or financial struggles—remind them you are in control. Please protect my friends and keep them safe. Guard their steps and all their ways.

Thank you for your protection, for being a strong tower when we feel like everything is crumbling around us.

In the name of Jesus, amen.

18

---

*God is our refuge and strength, a
very present help in trouble.*

PSALM 46:1

Lord Jesus, I praise you for your strength and protection. When I think about how strong you are compared to how weak I am, I'm overwhelmed. You alone are worthy of praise.

Remind me to focus on how big you are instead of how big my problems are. Remind me that you are my strong fortress and are always there for me to run to when life gets hard. I want to rest in your protection and not stress over things I can't control.

Peace and rest come from you. Remind my friends of that when they're too weary to carry on.

Thank you for loving and protecting me. You are my help when I'm in trouble, and I'm grateful I don't have to navigate life alone. You are always with me, and you've given me friends who walk beside me through life's valleys.

In the name of Jesus Christ, amen.

19

_____

So we may boldly say: "The LORD is my helper;
I will not fear. What can man do to me?"

HEBREWS 13:6

Prince of Peace, it's easy for me to be overwhelmed by the world. When I turn on the news, the headlines often cast fear over my day. But in the midst of that, I praise you because you are still in control.

Remind me who runs the universe. Remind me who sits on the throne. Let me not fear people or their evil plans. Instead, I want to hold tightly to the truth that nothing takes you by surprise.

Please protect my friends and give them confidence in you and your strength. Remind them that they don't have to be afraid but can boldly trust you, regardless of what's happening in their city or workplace or school.

Thank you for watching over my friends and me. Thank you for friends who take care of me in hard times. I'm grateful for heart-to-heart conversations with them when the world seems darkest.

In the holy name of Jesus, amen.

20

---

*Therefore submit to God. Resist the
devil and he will flee from you.*

Father God, you are trustworthy. You are the only one who never fails and never breaks a promise. You are worthy of my trust. And because I can trust you, I submit to you.

I want to live in a way that shows how much I trust you. I want to submit to you instead of making my own plans.

Help my friends see that trusting you is always best. It is tempting at times to go against your will or your plan, but that always leads to heartache and disaster. Protect my friends from rebelling against you, and give them soft hearts that will be swayed toward you and away from the evil that seeks to devour them.

Thank you for your Word and its instructions for handling moments of weakness and temptation. Thank you for being worthy of my trust. I'm so grateful for friends who remind me that your plan is always best.

In Jesus' name I pray, amen.

Prayers for Peace and Problem-Solving

21

*As iron sharpens iron, so a
friend sharpens a friend.*

PROVERBS 27:17 NLT

Heavenly Father, you are so good to your children. I love how you use little things in my day to shed light on what you're doing behind the scenes. You are worthy to be praised.

When iron rubs against iron, it grows sharper and becomes more effective. Help me sharpen my friends. I want to help prepare them for your purposes and your kingdom. I want to be a quality tool in your hands.

Sometimes being sharpened can be uncomfortable or even downright painful. Please give my friends grace during those difficult times. Help them develop and grow in grace and truth.

Thank you for giving me friends who make me a better person, friends who help me stay sharp and focused on what matters most.

In the name of your holy Son, amen.

22

Open rebuke is better than love carefully concealed. Faithful are the wounds of a friend, but the kisses of an enemy are deceitful.

Proverbs 27:5-6

Lord God, I know you discipline us because you love us. Thank you for showing your heart for your children this way. You've sent friends into my life to guide me along my journey, and they are priceless gifts to me.

When my friends give me wise counsel, help me receive it with a willing heart. Help me not shy away from their correction and instruction.

And please help my friends receive wisdom from me. Strengthen our friendships with hearts that always want the best for each other.

Thank you for friends who love me enough to tell the truth even when it's hard for me to hear.

In your Son's name, amen.

23

A troublemaker plants seeds of strife;
gossip separates the best of friends.

PROVERBS 16:28 NLT

Great God, you are so good to me. Healthy friendships are a gift from you, but the Enemy wants to separate those friendships with strife.

I ask that you sow peace in my relationships. When gossip tries to divide us, give me discernment to see the Enemy's trick and to stop it with a gentle response. I want always to speak of my friends as the treasures they are and never tear them down.

Help my friends recognize the severity of gossip in their lives. I ask that you protect our friendships from unkind words, rumors, and malicious talk. Let the words of their mouths glorify and honor you.

Thank you for the kind words my friends say to me. They build me up with their compassion and encouragement, which I know is a gift from you.

In Christ's name, amen.

24

Now we exhort you, brethren, warn those
who are unruly, comfort the fainthearted,
uphold the weak, be patient with all.

1 Thessalonians 5:14

Father, I praise you for your patience toward your people. You've blessed me in so many ways despite my impatience.

I want to trust your timing and not try to work things out on my own. When my friends are struggling to be patient, help me be there for them and guide them to trust your Word. Help me embrace your comfort and strength so I can pass it on to those I love.

My friends need your comfort, patience, and guidance. Let them find all they need in you, and equip them to be vessels of comfort, patience, and wisdom to others. Remind them that whatever problem they have is not too big for us to solve together with your guidance.

Thank you for being an example of love, comfort, and patience. I'm so grateful for my friends who show me how important those traits are and who inspire me to be better.

In the name of Jesus, amen.

25

---

*A hot-tempered person stirs up conflict, but
the one who is patient calms a quarrel.*

PROVERBS 15:18 NIV

Dear heavenly Father, Jesus is the ultimate example of peace in the face of persecution. He didn't defend himself or grow angry when tormented on the cross. Rather, he asked forgiveness for his persecutors.

Help me to do the same. Instead of being angry, I want to follow the example of Jesus and pray for those who injure me. I want to be like Jesus and be slow to anger, especially with my friends and those I love the most.

Some of my friends struggle with their tempers. Help them hold their tongues when they're tempted to give a hurtful response. Help them remember the example of Jesus.

Thank you for giving us the ability to choose peace over anger. Thank you that we don't have to give in to our natural desires. I'm so grateful my friends understand me and love me even when I'm not at my best.

In the name of your precious Son, amen.

26

"Let each one of you speak truth with his neighbor," for we are members of one another. "Be angry, and do not sin": do not let the sun go down on your wrath, nor give place to the devil.

EPHESIANS 4:25-27

Father God, I praise you because you are honest. You cannot lie, and you despise lying tongues.

I want to follow your example in this. I want to speak the truth always and in love. Help me resist the urge to lie when I'm caught doing something I shouldn't do. And I don't want to be guilty of lies of omission or lies to protect feelings.

When my friends are tempted to lie, give them the courage to be honest. Please guard our friendships, and let them always be built on truth, because we love one another and understand that lying never helps the situation.

Thank you for being an example of truth. I am so grateful I have friends who aren't afraid to tell me the truth.

In your Son's name, amen.

27

Pursue peace with all people, and holiness, without which no one will see the Lord: looking carefully lest anyone fall short of the grace of God; lest any root of bitterness springing up cause trouble, and by this many become defiled.

HEBREWS 12:14-15

Almighty God, I praise you for your heart for peace. Just as parents long for their children to love each other and get along, you desire for your people to live in peace with one another.

Help me not to harbor bitterness or unforgiveness toward my family or friends but to be an example of peacekeeping and holiness. I want to be someone who offers grace because of the grace I have received from you.

Be with my friends when they struggle with bitterness and unforgiveness. Help them let go of grudges and seek you instead of revenge. Remind them to pursue peace in all their relationships and not to give way to anger.

Thank you for friends who are comfortable telling me when they're angry with me so we can work things out. Thank you for your love for us and for your incredible blessings on our friendships.

In the holy name of Jesus, amen.

Prayers for Longevity and the Future

28

Don't be concerned for your own
good but for the good of others.

1 Corinthians 10:24 NLT

Dear God in heaven, I praise you for who you are and for the examples you give us in your Word. You sent Jesus to us as a perfect example of selflessness and heavenly love on earth.

It's easy to get caught up in my personal struggles and forget to put others first. Rid my heart of selfishness, and equip me to put my friends' interests before my own. Don't allow me to forget to minister to others in their struggles.

Bless and strengthen my friends. Give them an extra measure of your love, peace, and joy in the midst of their trials. Help us bless each other with acts of service and kindness.

Thank you that, through the work of the Holy Spirit, you make possible what seems impossible—being selfless.

In your name I pray, amen.

29

The Spirit Himself bears witness with our spirit that we are children of God, and if children, then heirs—heirs of God and joint heirs with Christ, if indeed we suffer with Him, that we may also be glorified together.

ROMANS 8:16-17

Heavenly Father, I praise you for your goodness and consistency toward your children. I don't deserve it, but you have made me an heir with Jesus because of your great love.

Help me today to remember my place. When I feel broken down and beat-up, remind me I am a child of God. When truth feels like a lie, help me not to doubt but to cling to your promises.

Remind my friends of their standing with you. When they struggle, whisper their names and reassure them that all the hardships will be worth it one day. Help them see that this life is temporary, but the eternal glory waiting for them will outweigh the bad times.

Thank you for calling me your child when I should be a servant.

In the name of the Most High King, Jesus, amen.

30

---

*Come now, you who say, "Today or
tomorrow we will go to such and such
a city, spend a year there, buy and sell,
and make a profit"; whereas you do not
know what will happen tomorrow.*

JAMES 4:13-14

Dear Lord, I praise you. Nothing slips through your hands. You are a God of organization and detail. You know it all, and you know what's best.

I often make plans and am disappointed when those plans fail. Help me trust in your plan and not in my own. Give me a desire to come to you first thing every morning and ask what you want me to do with my day.

Help my friends surrender their days to you. Help them see that you are directing their steps and that you are the best choreographer they could ask for. Remind them of your deep love for them and your attention to the details of their lives.

Thank you for watching over my friends and me. Thank you for always being right on time.

In the precious name of your Son, Jesus, amen.

31

---

*Do not forget my law, but let your heart
keep my commands; for length of days and
long life and peace they will add to you.*

PROVERBS 3:1-2

Father God, I praise you for your laws. Because of my rebellious nature, I don't always keep your commands. But your laws are good, and they are for my good.

Help me never to dismiss your commands. I want to be obedient to your Word. I know that when I am, I will experience joy and wellness of soul. Strengthen me to live out that desire to please you.

Be with my friends when they're tempted to sin against you. Remind them that keeping your law isn't just a good idea but is life and peace. Show them how they will thrive and flourish when they follow you and obey you.

Thank you for your laws. Your instructions always guide me to what's best. Your laws protect me from myself.

In the sweet name of Jesus, amen.

32

---

*Depend on the LORD in whatever you
do, and your plans will succeed.*

PROVERBS 16:3 NCV

Dear Father God, I praise you for your plan for my life. You are the God of the entire universe, yet you are so good to me and are involved in the details of my day.

Help me trust you with my day and every detail in it so I will walk with you and not go down my own path. I want my steps to be ordered by you so my mind will be at ease.

Help my friends trust that you are at work in their lives too. I pray that they will strive to honor you with every part of their day. As they commit their steps to you, give them peace and sureness of mind. Provide them with clarity so they don't have to wander aimlessly but instead will live with purpose.

Thank you for giving me friends who walk with me on this path through life. I look forward to every celebration and joyous moment to be shared.

In Jesus' name, amen.

33

Keep your lives free from the love of
money and be content with what you
have, because God has said, "Never will
I leave you; never will I forsake you."

Hebrews 13:5 NIV

Dear heavenly Father, you are the keeper of a thousand cattle on a thousand hills. You graciously provide for all your children's needs. I praise you for your provision!

I need to be reminded of this when I get discouraged about my finances. Help me not to stress over the balance in my bank account but to remember that you own it all and will take care of me.

Remind my friends that they can be confident of your provision. Keep them from feeling hopeless when bills pile up or the collectors call. Equip them to trust you even when it seems there is no way out of the situation.

Thank you for providing in your timing. I never have to doubt or worry if you're going to come through for me. Even when things don't make sense in the moment, I know you have a good plan.

In the name of your Son, amen.

Prayers for Love and Forgiveness

34

I, therefore, the prisoner of the Lord, beseech you to walk worthy of the calling with which you were called, with all lowliness and gentleness, with longsuffering, bearing with one another in love, endeavoring to keep the unity of the Spirit in the bond of peace.

EPHESIANS 4:1-3

Heavenly Father, you are so patient with me. I praise you for your patience toward me, for always bearing with me in love. You alone give peace that passes understanding.

Give me the grace to show that same love to my friends. Help me to be patient with them when we disagree and to demonstrate your gentleness and humility when my instinct is to demand my own way and my own opinion.

Help my friends embrace patience and peace. When we struggle to get along, give us the tools to work out our problems so we can show your love to others.

Thank you for calling me yours. Thank you for friends who understand that life can get hard and tempers can be short, but love between real friends lasts forever because of your blessing.

In your Son's name, amen.

35

---

*A father to the fatherless, a defender of
widows, is God in his holy dwelling.
God sets the lonely in families, he leads
out the prisoners with singing.*

PSALM 68:5-6 NIV

Abba Father, you are good to your children. There are many who no longer have their earthly parents, and you fill that role with your love. I praise you for the way you care specifically for each of your children.

I want to be the kind of friend who is closer than a brother. Help me meet the needs of those friends you've entrusted to me by being there for them completely and purely. Help me be the sibling they might feel they're missing in their lives.

I pray that my friends will sense your deep love for them. If they don't have earthly families, remind them of your provision and care. Let them embrace you as their father.

Sometimes family isn't born but chosen. Thank you for the friendships that mean as much to me as family does.

In Jesus' name, amen.

36

Love is patient, love is kind. It does not envy, it does not boast, it is not proud. It does not dishonor others, it is not self-seeking, it is not easily angered, it keeps no record of wrongs. Love does not delight in evil but rejoices with the truth. It always protects, always trusts, always hopes, always perseveres.

1 CORINTHIANS 13:4-7 NIV

Dear Jesus, you were and always will remain the ultimate example of true love. I praise you for your love for me even when I am so unlovable. Your love never fails.

I want to love purely and simply. I want to rejoice with my friends when they're happy, believe in them when they falter, and always hope for the best for them. Equip me to do this in your strength.

Help my friends find true love in you. Help them align their hearts with yours and be filled with love so they can pour it out on others.

Thank you that your love never runs out. Thank you that I have friends who show me love every day, whether it's through a timely text message, a funny social-media post, or a big hug.

In your precious name, amen.

37

If you bring your gift to the altar, and there remember that your brother has something against you, leave your gift there before the altar, and go your way. First be reconciled to your brother, and then come and offer your gift.

MATTHEW 5:23-24

Dear God in heaven, I praise you for your forgiving heart. You are the God of not only the second chance but also the third and fourth and fiftieth. Even though I don't deserve it, your love covers me, and your forgiveness washes me white as snow.

I don't want to hold grudges against a stranger, a family member, or my best friend. Show me how to forgive freely.

Help my friends forgive easily. When I hurt them, help them forgive me. When others speak harsh words or wrong them, remind my friends that forgiveness is the key to true freedom.

Thank you for being an example of forgiveness. When I feel it's too hard to forgive someone, I only have to think of your sacrifice to realize it is possible through you.

In the name of Jesus, amen.

38

For where two or three are gathered together in My name, I am there in the midst of them.

MATTHEW 18:20

Dear Jesus, you are sufficient. You are all we need in this life. Yet you still provide friendships and human love that help fill the empty places. I praise you for providing for our need for community and fellowship.

Remind me that there is power in numbers. Help me not withdraw when I feel discouraged, but instead prompt me to be vulnerable and open with my friends and invite them into my hurt or pain. Your Word promises that when we pray together, things happen!

Remind my friends that they are never alone. Help them to be bold in admitting their need for you and for others. And help them to freely ask for prayer.

Thank you for never leaving me alone, and thank you for loving me through my friends. Because of them, I often feel your presence in new ways.

In your name I pray, amen.

39

---

*A person's friends should be kind
to him when he is in trouble.*

JOB 6:14 NCV

Dear heavenly Father, I praise you for your attention to me when I go through painful times. You never leave me but continue to show your great love for me in the darkest days.

When life is sunny, remind me that my friends may be struggling with shadows. Don't let me be so caught up in my own life that I forget to pray for and care for them.

Encourage my friends today in the midst of their hardships and trials. Help them show others the kind of friendship they want to receive. Remind them to be kind in all their relationships and not be just fair-weather friends.

Thank you for friends who meet my needs, for friends who celebrate with me over job promotions and new relationships, and for friends who mourn with me when I go through layoffs or breakups.

In the name of Jesus, amen.

40

Be kind to one another, tenderhearted,
forgiving one another, even as
God in Christ forgave you.

Ephesians 4:32

Dear heavenly Father, you are so good to me. You forgive me, love me, and are kind to me. You are the perfect example of how to love others when it can be hard.

Some days it seems easier to hold a grudge and be upset than to offer forgiveness or be tenderhearted toward my friends. Remind me that I don't deserve forgiveness but, because of Christ, I have it anyway.

Help my friends have a forgiving heart when I hurt them. Prompt them to be tenderhearted toward me and to remember that gentle answers turn away anger but harsh words escalate the situation.

Thank you for providing me with friends who see the best in me even when I don't see it myself. Thank you for friends who are willing to forgive because they have been forgiven first by you. What a gift they are to me.

In the sweet name of Jesus, amen.

About Max Lucado

More than 120 million readers have found inspiration and encouragement in the writings of Max Lucado. He lives with his wife, Denalyn, and their mischievous mutt, Andy, in San Antonio, Texas, where he serves the people of Oak Hills Church. Visit his website at MaxLucado.com or follow him at Twitter.com/MaxLucado and Facebook.com/MaxLucado.

About Betsy St. Amant

Betsy St. Amant is the author of fourteen contemporary novels and novellas. She resides in north Louisiana with her story-telling daughter, a collection of Austen novels, and an impressive stash of Pickle Pringles. Betsy has a B.A. in Communications and a deep-rooted passion for seeing women set free in Christ. Her latest novel with HarperCollins is *Love Arrives in Pieces*. Visit her at www.betsystamant.com.

Discover Even More Power in a Simple Prayer

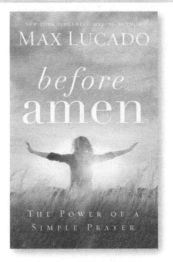

ISBN 978-0-7180-7812-6

$15.99

Join Max Lucado on a journey to the very heart of biblical prayer and discover rest in the midst of chaos and confidence even for prayer wimps.

Available wherever books are sold.

BeforeAmen.com

Make Your Prayers Personal

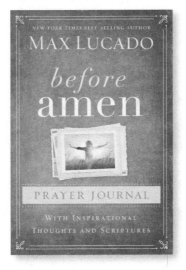

ISBN 978-0-7180-1406-3

$13.99

This beautiful companion journal to *Before Amen* helps readers stoke their prayer life. It features quotes and scriptures to inspire both prayer warriors and those who struggle to pray.

Tools for Your Church and Small Group

Before Amen: A DVD Study

ISBN 978-0-529-12342-8

$21.99

Max Lucado leads this four-session study through his discovery of a simple tool for connecting with God each day. This study will help small-group participants build their prayer life, calm the chaos of their world, and grow in Christ.

Before Amen Study Guide

ISBN 978-0-529-12334-3

$9.99

This guide is filled with Scripture study, discussion questions, and practical ideas designed to help small-group members understand Jesus' teaching on prayer. An integral part of the *Before Amen* small-group study, it will help group members build prayer into their everyday lives.

Before Amen
Church Campaign Kit

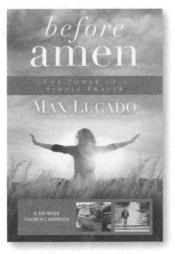

ISBN 978-0-529-12369-5

$49.99

The church campaign kit includes a four-session DVD study by Max Lucado; a study guide with discussion questions and video notes; the *Before Amen* trade book; a getting started guide; and access to a website with all the sermon resources churches need to launch and sustain a four-week *Before Amen* campaign.

Before Amen for Everyone

Before Amen Audiobook

ISBN 978-1-4915-4662-8 | $19.99

Enjoy the unabridged audio CD of *Before Amen*.

Before Amen eBook

ISBN 978-0-529-12390-9

Read *Before Amen* anywhere on your favorite tablet or electronic device.

Antes del amén Spanish Edition

ISBN 978-0-7180-0157-5 | $13.99

The hope of *Before Amen* is also available for Spanish-language readers.